# A PASSION FOR
# CAVIAR

## THE ART OF EATING AND ENJOYING

# A PASSION FOR
# CAVIAR

## THE ART OF EATING AND ENJOYING

**SUSIE BOECKMANN &
NATALIE REBEIZ-NIELSEN**

MITCHELL
BEAZLEY

**Notes**

Both metric and imperial measurements have been given in all recipes.

Use one set of measurements only and not a mixture of both.

Standard level spoon measurements are used in all recipes.

Eggs should be size 3 unless otherwise stated.

Milk should be full fat unless otherwise stated.

Ovens should be preheated to the specified temperature - if using a fan assisted oven, follow the manufacturer's instructions for adjusting the time and the temperature.

Art Director: **Jacqui Small**

Executive Art Editor: **Penny Stock**

Executive Editor: **Susan Haynes**

Editor: **Sasha Judelson**

Photography: **James Merrell**

Stylist: **Sue Skeen**

Home Economist: **Bridget Sargeson**

First published in Great Britain in 1995
by Mitchell Beazley
an imprint of Reed International Books Limited
Michelin House, 81 Fulham Road, London SW3 6RB
and Auckland and Melbourne. Reprinted 1997.

ISBN 1 85732 628 8
A CIP catalogue record for this book is available from the
British Library.

Produced by Mandarin Offset
Printed and bound in China

Our heartfelt thanks go to Hanne Sorensen who co-ordinated and kept us under control, always with a smile; to all those in Caviar House who gave us their support and information and all the other people in the caviar industry who helped contribute; to Dr Alwyne Wheeler, formerly of the British Museum (Natural History) and finally to our patient husbands and children. Hopefully you will find our dishes attractive and delicious, to tickle your taste buds without making your pockets too bare.

# INTRODUCTION

There are now three main kinds of caviar sold commercially, although there are over 400 different species of sturgeon worldwide. It is only in the Caspian that the unique combination of optimum water temperatures, climate and rivers running into the sea come together to create the perfect conditions for this fish; the caviar of the Caspian sturgeon is acknowledged to be the best in the world. There are many other parts of the world where caviar is produced, but it never consistently equals the quality of the Caspian variety. The largest of the fish is the Beluga, followed by the Oscietre and then the Sevruga. Not long ago there was also Sterlet and Schipp but these two are no longer caught in sufficient quantities to be sold commercially. There is also the very rare golden caviar (generally agreed to be the Albino Oscietre or Beluga) which it was the right of the Czars of Russia and the Shahs of Iran to consume. Any commoner caught eating this rare delicacy in Iran was liable to lose his right hand! Today we can sometimes obtain this type of caviar but it is very rare, and so extremely expensive.

The sturgeon is a migratory fish, generally swimming up river to spawn and returning to the sea every year, although there are exceptions to this: some sturgeon have adapted to staying solely in rivers or the sea. Also many sturgeon species interbreed with each other which has sometimes made identifying different species rather difficult.

The spurned wife of a movie mogul in Hollywood took to bathing in caviar when her husband fell for a young, beautiful actress. Her first reason for doing this was that she really believed that caviar would keep her skin soft and youthful; the second that she paid with his credit card which gave her an even bigger boost!

# CAVIAR CURIOSITIES

## Russian Caviar

Russian caviar has always had a wonderful reputation. In 1893 the Russians made an agreement with Iran to purchase, process and import all the Iranian sturgeon catch. This resulted in the Iranians being forced to sell to them at vastly reduced prices and lasted until 1952 when each party agreed fishing rights and became independent.

Unfortunately for the past five or six years, since the dissolution of the U.S.S.R. there has been a breakdown in controlling the previously strict quotas on sturgeon catches. It is no longer the State which controls the caviar market, making sure that it is produced in prime condition. This has led to a great deal of poaching and illegal fishing.

Powerful local mafias have gained control of the fishing stations in many areas because caviar is such a valuable commodity and is dealt in much desired Western currencies. Consequently those in the established caviar industry often come across eggs which are not properly cleaned or preserved and moreover are sold in fake tins designed to resemble the official state packaging.

Despite attempts to prevent overfishing, such as the two frigates and 300 soldiers patrolling the Volga tributeries, the Beluga is nearly extinct; if controls are not brought in soon it will cease to exist.

This once famous Russian delicacy has recently been overtaken by Iran, which now produces a fine quality product with modern factories and European health standards.

## Is there any difference between Russian and Iranian Caviar?

The fish are caught in the same sea but there are differences in the processing of the caviar. Russian caviar tends to have more salt added than Iranian and the Russians add a little borax to the salt which enhances the flavour, preserves the caviar for longer and sweetens the eggs a little. This also makes the eggs a bit oilier.

The Iranians process with pure salt at around 2.5% per kilo as opposed to 4% per kilo in Russia.

## History

The sturgeon is a prehistoric fish; fossil remains dating from that time have been found on the Baltic coast and elsewhere.

Around 2400 BC the ancient Egyptian and Phoenician coastal dwellers knew how to salt and pickle fish and eggs, to last them in times of war, famine or on long sea voyages. There are some bas-reliefs at the Necropolis near to the Sakkara Pyramid which show fisherman catching all kinds of fish, gutting them and removing their eggs.

Writing in the 4th century BC, Aristotle declared sturgeon flesh delicious and described how a gelatin made from the swim bladder was used as a strong glue and for clarifying wine. (It is called isinglas and is still used today for these same purposes, and also in optics; the Chinese dry the product for use in soup.) When Rome was at the height of its prosperity from the 4th century BC onwards, many writers and philosophers including Pliny, Cicero, Ovid and Athenaeus wrote of sturgeon.

In the Middle Ages shoals of sturgeon were to be found in the Thames, Seine, Po and Ebro Rivers and the upper stretches of the Danube. At this time sovereigns of many countries, including Russia, China, Denmark, France and England had claimed the rights to sturgeon. Fishermen had to offer the catch to the sovereign, often for fixed rewards.

In Russia and Hungary the sections of rivers considered suitable for fishing the great sturgeon (the Beluga as we know it) were the subject of special royal grants. Under the Czar's benevolence the Cossacks of the Dnieper, the Don and the Ural were allowed to fish for one fortnight twice a year, in the spring (Bagornaja catch) and autumn (Plawnaja catch).

Apart from the Cossacks and their families, the river banks were crowded with rich dealers from Moscow, Leningrad and parts of Europe. The fresh fish were sold to the highest bidder, who then had the fish killed, prepared the caviar on the spot, and then packed it in barrels filled with ice to be transported. The Cossacks continued to have the right to sturgeon fishing until the Russian Revolution in 1917.

## Aphrodite's Eggs

Aphrodite is the Goddess of Love. Coming from the sea she epitomizes love, passion and health, making caviar and other seafood the ideal food for lovers. It should be treated as such.

There's no scientific proof that caviar is an aphrodisiac, but its stimulating properties are incontestable - from old Russian poetry to ancient Persian and Indian stories, caviar has always been lauded for its 'exciting virtues' in seduction.

## Health and Nutrition

Caviar is light, full of vitamins, low in calories and almost a complete food in itself.

Russia has known of the health benefits of caviar for centuries, and it is used today to prevent rickets in children. It is also given to patients after surgery to aid their recovery, as apart from its high protein content it is easy to consume and digest. Caviar is believed to increase the life span of the consumer.

Caviar is also good for hangovers as it contains acetylcholine which increases tolerance to alcohol. Russians extract the oil from the eggs and drink it as we would drink cod liver oil, and use it to line their stomachs before hitting the vodka.

## Beauty Treatments

Some people like to bathe in caviar, and it has been used as a beauty product by several cosmetic companies.

Beauticians have been known to use caviar for a nourishing face mask by extracting the essential oils from the eggs. The testes of the male sturgeon is made into a balm to soothe and cure burns.

A certain chic Parisian lady launched *Perles du Caviar* in the 1980s. It felt great on the skin but smelt awful! A Manhattan hair salon made a solution of caviar and clay to condition dry bleached hair. It was said to be very popular. Bloomingdales stock a caviar extract rejuvenating cream for the eyes and throat, which is sold at $35 for half an ounce! A chemist in West London once extracted the oils from caviar and mixed them to a secret formula which he marketed as a rejuvenating cream.

A Scotsman dining at the Waldorf Astoria for the first time, with a new girl-friend asked what was the most expensive dish on the menu. The waiter replied 'Caviar, Sir' – 'What is that?' enquired the man. 'Fish eggs, Sir' – 'We will have one each fried sunny side up, waiter' ordered the careful gentleman.

# APPEARANCES

## Good

**Tins** should be vacuum packed with a tight seal. To break the seal it should be necessary to take a coin to the tin edge to break the vacuum. Any rubber bands on tins should be removed with a knife. Lift the lid carefully – the tin should be firmly packed with eggs.

**Caviar** should have a healthy, glossy, slightly oily appearance. The eggs should all be separate, round and firm (but not hard).

**Smell** your eggs - there should be a slight aroma of the sea - never a strong odour.

**To** taste, put a little caviar on the back of your hand in the 'V' between your thumb and forefinger. Eat it from the skin, rolling the eggs in your mouth and then gently popping them to release their full flavour (which will vary from variety to variety and fish to fish). Then rub the skin on your hand; there should be no remaining smell.

**If** your caviar has been frozen, you can try a rescue job. Either thaw it slowly in the refrigerator or transfer the eggs to a fine non-metal (preferably silk-meshed) sieve.

**When** buying good caviar packed in glass, turn the jar around slowly: the eggs should follow the jar around.

**If** you buy caviar from a good retailer (unless you are buying the original blue 1.8 kg/4 lb tins) you will usually find that Beluga is in blue labelled tins, Oscietre in yellow, and Sevruga in red.

**Tins** of caviar can be kept in a refrigerator for about 2-3 months at a temperature of 3°C/37°F. A professional will keep tins for up to a year at a temperature of between -3°C/26°F and -5°C/22°F. Larger tins should be turned from time to time to redistribute the natural oils evenly.

## Bad

**The** vacuum seal should never be broken. This would mean that the tin was not properly sealed, allowing air to get in and destroy the eggs. It could also mean that the tin had been opened by someone else, either to repack the contents or even to change them to something other than that specified on the lid. The tin should always be full (regardless of size); if it is not, the contents are likely to have been incorrectly packed or processed.

**If** there is anything other than eggs and a little oil in your caviar - such as bits of membrane, specks of blood or occasionally white crystals around the eggs - return the tin to the retailer immediately.

**If** the eggs smell tart, acidic or fishy – they are not fresh.

**When** caviar is old it becomes much saltier. If eggs have a strong fishy flavour or slight ammonia-like taste they are not fresh.

**If** caviar does not move around the jar be suspicious - it is probably low grade, too old, and has become dry.

**Black** market caviar can come in any tin although the packaging will usually resemble that used for well-known brands.

**Never** open a tin of caviar without checking the sell-by date.

**Glass** jars often have a magnifying effect on eggs so your eggs may look bigger than they are actually are.

In the United States at the beginning of this
century, before prohibition, there was such an
abundance of caviar that it was given away free in
New York bars to encourage greater beer
consumption, being rather salty.

# CAVIAR VARIETIES

The three prominent varieties of caviar sold are Beluga, Sevruga and Oscietre and these are the varieties you are most likely to eat and buy. We have discussed these caviars overleaf, together with Golden or Imperial caviar. The caviars produced from other sturgeon are interesting to compare to the main caviars in terms of flavour and production methods. Many countries produce fake eggs out of fish products with oils, gelatine and flavourings, which when processed resemble fish eggs. By using dyes and artificial flavourings the size and colour of an egg can be regulated to resemble almost any fish egg from salmon to sturgeon.

### STERLET

*(Acipenser Linnaeus Ruthenus)*

The Sterlet is similar but smaller than the average Sevruga. It has been known to reach 1.25 metres/4 ft and weigh as much as 16 kg/35 lb, but normally the fish does not grow to more than 1 metre/39 inches in length and weighs 6-6½ kg/13-14 lb. In the past Sterlet (mainly a river sturgeon) accounted for over 50% of the catch from the mouth of the Volga. Fifty years ago 700 tons were caught in a year, but now it is very rare.

The largest remaining population of the Sterlet is in Yugoslavia, then Bulgaria, Rumania, Czechoslovakia and Hungary. Although it is no longer caught for commercial caviar purposes, the Sterlet is a very important fish as far as propagation is concerned, breeding and crossbreeding successfully in warm water with other species of sturgeon. This fact makes it a vital member of the sturgeon family for the future.

Historically, the Sterlet has featured in all kinds of feasts and banquets; Sterlet caviar soup seems to have been popular.

### SCHIPP CAVIAR

This is sometimes sold commercially. The flavour is somewhere between Sevruga and Oscietre but the eggs are often less firm than either of these. Sometimes the eggs are graded as Oscietre or Sevruga depending on the size caught. Schipp is the result of crossbreeding between the Sterlet and Sevruga.

### PRESSED CAVIAR

Pressed caviar is compressed eggs mainly taken from damaged Sevruga or Oscietre sturgeon, resulting in a strong salty fishy flavour. It is not so popular today but is highly appreciated by traditional caviar experts and is easy to cook with.

### MALOSSOL

The word 'malossol' means lightly salted in Russian and traditionally only eggs in prime condition are prepared and labelled this way. It takes great expertise to judge precisely the stage at which a sturgeon's eggs are absolutely right for this process: so beware! The eggs may not contain more than 2.8-3% salt. In Europe a very small amount of borax is added to the salt (many experts believe this improves and slightly sweetens the caviar) but this is not permitted in the U.S. Iran also uses only pure salt for processing.

'Malossol' has wrongly come to mean any high quality caviar.

### PASTEURISED CAVIAR

Russia went into pasteurising caviar seriously around the time of the First World War, and remains the only country to produce it. It was so cold then that fishing became impossible. Rather than lose their established markets they poured their existing stocks of caviar into huge 500 litre/104 gallon barrels, covered the tops and left them in a very hot room to cook.

Today's methods are much more effective, jars of caviar are properly sealed and put into water baths with a constant temperature of about 60°C/140°C.

The glass jars commonly used to package Pasteurised Caviar can have the effect of magnifying the eggs when viewed from the outside, which is why so much is falsely sold as Beluga.

### CHINESE CAVIAR

There are several species of sturgeon found in China, mainly in the Amur and Liman rivers. Most commonly known as the Kaluga, the eggs are often unfortunately very salty and because of the fishing methods used do not have consistent quality.

### IMPERIAL OR GOLDEN CAVIAR

Golden caviar used to be reserved for the Czars of Russia, Emperors of Manchuria and even the Vatican. Latterly in Iran it was kept exclusively for the Shah. Caviar experts have many theories as to what golden caviar actually is. The biggest caviar company believes that golden caviar comes from an Oscietre fish that is over 60 years old. At that point the eggs change to a pale golden colour and the flavour becomes smooth, creamy and delicate.

Another popular theory is that golden caviar comes from an albino fish - Beluga or Oscietre (and in the past from the Sterlet as well). The eggs are an off-white colour. Albino caviar commands a very high price because of its rarity. The flavour is not nearly so good as that of the pale Oscietre eggs.

**Pictured right**

### OSCIETRE

*(Acipencer Guldenstadtii)*

The Oscietre sturgeon is in some ways the most interesting of the sturgeon, as it has the widest variety of eggs in terms of size, colour and taste. The average mature fish grows to 1.5 metres/4¾ ft and weighs between 20 and 80 kg/44 and 176 lb. It has a short thick head with a slightly pointed nose and small mouth through which it sucks up plants, small fish and crustacea. It also has two sets of barbels above its mouth, these are important feelers when the fish is feeding on the bottom of the seabed. The Oscietre produces eggs from 12-15 years of age. When young the eggs are large and mostly of a dark golden shade. As the fish ages the roe fades to a pale amber and has a subtle flavour. Some say that the taste differs so much because the fish dives to the sea-bottom to avoid fishermen. It buries itself under algae and mud. The camouflage it chooses may affect the flavour.

**Pictured left**

## BELUGA
### (Huso Huso)

The Beluga is the biggest of the sturgeons and the only one that is exclusively carnivorous. It is so rare that it is unusual for more than 100 to be caught per year in the Caspian waters.

The Beluga is a silvery grey colour and differs from other sturgeon in that it loses the bony scales along its length when it is a few months old. It has a big short head with a pointed snout and large mouth and two sets of barbels under its mouth.

The mouth of a full-grown Beluga sturgeon may be up to 25 cm/10 inches wide and the fish has been known to swallow whole salmon. It is also the fastest swimmer of the sturgeon family, enabling it to follow shoals of shad, herring, mullet and other white fish.

Up to 25% of the Beluga's body weight may consist of eggs, and individual fish have been known to carry up to 50% eggs. The female fish matures only when it is 25-40 years old, and may not spawn every year.

The female Beluga is highly prized for its large grained egg with a fine skin. The colour varies from light grey to nearly black. The lightest grey is particularly prized.

**Pictured right**

## SEVRUGA
### (Acipenser Stellatus)

The Sevruga is the smallest sturgeon used commercially. It grows to a maximum of 1.5 metres/4¾ ft and seldom exceeds 25 kg/55 lb. It has a snub nose with a long snout and two sets of barbels, just above its small mouth. Like the Oscietre it is an omnivore and bottom-feeds on algae and crustacea. It has very distinctive bony scales which resemble stars.

The female Sevruga starts producing eggs from about 7-10 years of age; around 10-12% of her body weight are eggs. Most of the fish caught are 8-22 years old, when the eggs are probably at their best.

The eggs are grey black with a fine grain. They are small and the most salty to taste. Amongst connoisseurs they are highly appreciated for their unique flavour. They are also the least expensive source of caviar, mainly because there are more of them and they produce eggs at an earlier age.

**Pictured left**

## EGGS FROM OTHER SOURCES

Other fish eggs eaten include cod, herring, flying fish, pike, carp, pollack, flounder, mackerel and some species of crab. In most countries fish eggs should only be labelled caviar if they come from sturgeon from the Caspian Sea, but there are exceptions to this and some countries, including America, use the word caviar together with the name of the fish which yielded the roe, such as lumpfish caviar or salmon caviar.

### SALMON EGGS/KETA

These are large naturally orange/red coloured eggs about the size of a small pea. They have a strong salmon 'yolky' flavour and should melt in the mouth. The eggs should be a good round shape and when squeezed should not break. There is not much difference between pasteurised and unpasteurised salmon eggs.

Several kinds of salmon are used for their eggs but the most common in Europe is Keta and in America Chum, pink or sockeye. Japan and Russia are by far the largest producers and consumers of salmon eggs in the world.

**Pictured right**

### FISH EGGS (AMERICAN)

These come from a variety of fish. They can be natural, coloured or flavoured according to market requirements.

**Pictured left**

### LUMPFISH

As its name suggests this is an ugly lumpy fish, found mainly in Scandinavian waters. It weighs between 2-7 kg/ 4-15 lb; some 15-30% of its body weight consists of eggs.

The eggs are a small grain roe which come in a whole rainbow of different colours. They are normally dyed dark grey/black to resemble Sevruga caviar, or sometimes red. Lumpfish is widely used as a garnish for soups and canapés instead of 'real' caviar. It has a slightly fishy, salty taste and the eggs are slightly crunchy to eat.

### MULLET EGGS

These are the oldest recorded dried and processed eggs, predating sturgeon. Today they are still widely sold as *Botarga* (with spelling varying). The eggs are salted, dried and then preserved in a translucent wax casing.

### TROUT EGGS

A smaller grained orange egg about half the size of a salmon egg.

Enthusiastic anglers take the eggs from the trout they catch, wash the roe in milk, then rinse them in water several times. Salt and a little sugar are added before draining the roe as much as possible on kitchen paper. The roe needs then to go into a bowl to be pressed with a weight for 24 hours.

Pressed roe spread on toast is quite delicious.

**Pictured right**

### TUNA EGGS

In Europe tuna is caught off the west coasts of Sardinia and Sicily and in central Mediterranean waters. Spawning occurs from April to June when the water becomes warmer. Traditionally tuna eggs were first extracted and then divided among the crews. Today tuna eggs are vacuum packed to retain their taste and fragrance. They should be taken out of their container a couple of hours before serving.

### SEA URCHIN EGGS

The most expensive seafood egg comes from *oursin*, a type of black spiny sea urchin considered a great delicacy amongst fish eating connoisseurs. These are now a protected species in some Mediterranean waters. They are collected in the summer months in deep rocky waters and when cut open reveal a bright orange mass of very small eggs, which have a very delicate taste and fine slightly grainy texture.

### AMERICAN CAVIAR

This comes mainly from the farmed 'paddlefish' (not a true sturgeon). There are strict laws regarding processing and selling. It has a poor flavour compared with Caspian caviar.

**Pictured left**

There are several other species of sturgeon and fish eggs which we have not covered as you are not likely to come across them in commercial or retail outlets.

# HOW TO SERVE CAVIAR

Of course, you can eat your caviar from a simple glass bowl, using a plastic spoon - but artists through history have been inspired by the rarity and expense of caviar. Fabergé created spoons of gold, malachite, lapis lazuli and amber; others were inspired to use mother-of-pearl, tortoiseshell or polished wood. Two early gold and silversmiths, Paul de Lamerie and Paul Storr, each designed and made beautiful solid silver caviar servers with inner dishes lined in gold. Old Russian and French silversmiths have also paid homage to caviar - even Louis Vuitton has a marvellous caviar picnic set. Lalique also have some fine examples of caviar dishes in their exquisite glass.

Today you can find spoons, scoops and caviar knives made of mother-of-pearl, wood or horn (usually deer, cattle or rams' horn). They come in many sizes and shapes but should be as smooth as your caviar! Some are simple, others carved or with handles decorated in silver or gold.

Note: Horn spoons are used most often today but to retain their lustre they should not be washed in dishwashers or with hot water or detergents. Wipe clean with vinegar and kitchen paper, rinse under warm water and dry carefully.

## Notes on Serving

Take your caviar out of the refrigerator 10-15 minutes to an hour before serving, but do not open the tin or jar until the last minute.

Remember caviar's enemies – air and heat!

Use bone, mother of pearl, gold plated or even plastic spoons - never use stainless steel or silver: or your caviar will rapidly change its flavour and oxidise. Plastic is better than metal because (unlike many more exotic and attractive materials), it does not carry a taste, is unaffected by acids, vinegar or oils and does not stain.

If you have a special caviar dish put crushed ice in the outer bowl, keep it chilled and add the caviar at the last minute. If you have not got a special caviar serving bowl you can simply put the tin or jar in a glass bowl of crushed ice. Scoop caviar out of the tin vertically from top to bottom, never horizontally as this might crush the grains.

Serve directly on individual plates.

Caviar should never be exposed to the air for more than one hour.

## How much do you need?

Allow 25-50 g/1-2 oz caviar per person. It is quite a good idea to buy the amount you require in two tins rather than purchasing one large tin, just in case you do not use it all. If unopened, the second tin can be kept for another occasion. This makes sense because once opened, caviar must be consumed within two or three days and after all there are some people who do not like it (more for us!).

# WHAT TO DRINK WITH CAVIAR

The Russians are the largest consumers of caviar and vodka is the national drink so this creates a natural bond between the two – both for celebrations and for everyday. There is a large choice of excellent vodkas to be found at good wine merchants today. They will advise you, or you can experiment with all kinds of flavours.

One of the most popular vodka's in Natalie's shop is a pepper–flavoured vodka. Otherwise go for a classic Stolichnaya. Vodka should be served very cold. If you keep your vodka in the freezer it will not freeze because of the alcohol content, but when poured it will come out like a syrup. On the other hand there are those who prefer a champagne or a dry white wine. A good crisp white burgundy such as a Chablis or a Pouilly Fuisse (or Fumé) is delicious with caviar as are some of the 'New World' Chardonnays, but avoid the really oaky ones as they are too rich and fruity for caviar. As caviar is normally served as an event, to seduce, to impress, or just because you like it, it is important to have the drink of your choice, that you enjoy the most. In the end it is as with caviar: always your personal taste.

**The number of caviar tins or glass jars packed per year is approximately 1,100,000.**

# A LITTLE GUIDANCE

There are many misconceptions regarding caviar and one of the commonest questions asked is: 'Which is the best?'

To people in the caviar business that is really like asking if you prefer sole, salmon or trout - it depends on your choice or the prevailing circumstances: perhaps your dealer has a better Oscietre than Sevruga on the date of purchase or vice versa.

It would be unwise to put Beluga on canapés at a large reception as the delicate flavour would probably not be appreciated by a chatty crowd knocking back a variety of drinks in a smoky room. On the other hand, a romantic dinner for two would be an ideal occasion to enjoy the creamy delicate flavour. With its stronger flavour, Sevruga would be excellent on small canapés.

Many people also insist that 'a black Beluga with very large eggs' is the best, whereas others state with equal conviction that a grey egg is the only good colour. There really is no difference in the quality. The colour of the eggs comes from the individual fish.

Caviar should be judged by its quality and taste and not by the price. People tend to think that the most expensive is the best, but this is not necessarily true. Many connoisseurs would prize a new season Sevruga with its long distinctive nose, small eggs, and delicate but strongish flavour above all others. The French, who are the biggest European consumers of caviar, eat the most Oscietre. Some members of the older generation, Eastern Europeans and Russians would prefer pressed caviar.

**The Queen's Grill on the Queen Elizabeth II serves 15% of the world's consumption of Beluga caviar.**

# THE RECIPES

The best way to eat good caviar is by itself with perhaps thin white toast, blinis or waxy new potatoes, but because it is rare and expensive we have tried to create a selection of different dishes to suit every occasion and have not used any recipes that we don't like ourselves. With all the recipes we suggest, you can of course change the type of caviar to suit your taste, pocket or gift. The only proviso being that if you are adding caviar to a hot sauce Sevruga eggs are the most suitable as they can withstand a certain amount of cooking. Beluga eggs are too delicate and will burst and leave your dish a rather muddy colour. If you are enclosing eggs in a dish you can get away with an Oscietre, as the centre of the dish is not cooked for long enough to destroy the caviar in the middle.

You do not have to be tied to most recipes. Fromage frais, soured cream, crème fraîche - it is all a question of what you prefer. But be aware that sour cream is usually runnier than the other two so if coating or spreading it on a canapé it is better to use crème fraîche or fromage frais.

We do not feel that lemon juice should be added to caviar with the exception of pasteurised caviar, because this can oxidise it.

For many people the perfect combination is a baked potato with caviar. You can create this dish with potatoes of any size. Bake the potatoes in a preheated oven, 180°C (350°F), Gas Mark 4, for 1-2 hours, depending on their size. Split the potatoes down the centre and squeeze to open them up. Spoon crème fraîche or soured cream into the centre of each. Sprinkle with chopped red onion and top with caviar.

# CAVIAR
## WITH TRADITIONAL ACCOMPANIMENTS & BLINIS

This way of serving caviar probably originated in Europe and America, supposedly introduced to mask the taste of rancid or salty caviar. Although it is no longer necessary to take such steps it does make your caviar go further. Some shops and supermarkets that sell caviar now sell blinis.

**2 eggs**

**2 tablespoons of finely chopped parsley**

**I large red onion, very finely chopped**

**40-50 g/1½-2 oz caviar of your choice per person**

**150 ml/¼ pint soured cream**

**I lemon, quartered (optional)**

First make your blinis, following the recipe of your choice (see pp 30-31). These may be made in advance and kept covered in the refrigerator or frozen until about one hour before using. Heat just before serving.

Put the eggs in a pan of cold salted water. Bring to the boil, reduce the heat and simmer for 10 minutes, then drain, cool under cold running water and drain again. Set aside.

Shell the eggs and carefully remove the yolks. Chop both whites and yolks finely, keeping them separate.

Arrange the hard-boiled egg whites, yolks, parsley and onion around the rim of four individual plates, leaving the centre free for the caviar, which should be added just before serving. The soured cream may be put on the plate or passed around in a bowl. If you must, add a lemon wedge to each portion.

Pass around the warm blinis, allowing several per person, depending on the size.

Serves 4

**In Russia caviar was perfectly commonplace;**
**the Tsar's children used to eat**
**mashed banana and caviar for breakfast.**

# BLINIS

Nice and easy for busy working people; you do not need a blini pan to make these big thick blinis.

**200 g/7 oz plain flour, sifted**

**¼ teaspoon salt**

**3 eggs**

**400 ml/14 fl oz semi-skimmed milk**

**50 g/2 oz butter**

**caviar, to serve**

Prepare the batter. Combine the flour, salt, eggs and milk in a blender or food processor. Process for 1-2 minutes until smooth. Alternatively, combine the dry ingredients in a large bowl, make a well in the centre and add the beaten eggs and milk to the well. Gradually incorporate the flour, stirring until smooth. Whichever method you choose, strain the batter through a sieve into a jug and let it stand for 30 minutes.

Melt the butter in a small saucepan, and pour a little into a large nonstick frying pan. Pour enough of the batter into the pan to make four blinis (small pancakes), each about 5 mm/¼ inch thick. Allow them to cook for about 10 minutes on each side over a moderate heat.

When the blinis are cooked, transfer them to a wire rack, piling them loosely on top of each other to keep them moist. Keep them warm in a low oven while making four more blinis, remembering to add a little more melted butter to the pan when necessary.

Serve the blinis warm, with caviar.

Makes 8

# BLINI WITH BUCKWHEAT AND PLAIN FLOUR

**250-300 ml/8-10 fl oz milk**

**1½ teaspoons dried yeast or 10 g/⅓ oz fresh yeast**

**4 tablespoons lukewarm water, if using fresh yeast**

**50 g/2 oz plain flour**

**100 g/3½ oz buckwheat flour**

**½ teaspoon salt**

**50 g/2 oz butter (maybe a bit more when cooking blinis)**

**2 eggs, separated**

**2 tablespoons soured cream**

**caviar, to serve**

Pour 175 ml/6 fl oz of the milk into a pan. Heat until the milk rises, remove from the heat and allow it to cool. Mix the fresh yeast with the water. Leave for 5 minutes until the surface is covered in bubbles. Sift the flours and salt into a bowl. Mix thoroughly. Add the dried yeast, if using then make a well. Add the fresh yeast and lukewarm milk to the well. Gradually incorporate the flour. Beat for 2 minutes until smooth. Cover with a damp tea towel and put in a warm place for 2-3 hours until risen and full of bubbles. Melt half the butter in a pan and allow to cool a little. Add a further 50 ml/2 fl oz of the milk to the risen batter, stir it in thoroughly. Stir in the egg yolks, soured cream and melted butter until the mixture has the consistency of double cream. (If it seems too thick to pour, add a little more milk.)

Whisk the egg whites until stiff peaks form. Fold the egg whites into the batter, a little at a time, cutting and folding into the batter until thoroughly mixed in. Heat half the remaining butter in a frying pan. Pour enough batter into the pan to make small blinis. Cook for 1-2 minutes, turning when lightly browned. Add more butter to the pan as necessary until all the batter is used. Serve warm, with caviar.

*Serves 8*

# TÊTE-À-TÊTE

This romantic breakfast for 'the morning after' is highly nutritious, full of protein and should heighten your energy buzz enormously.

**2 very fresh free range eggs**

**2 heaped teaspoons soured cream or fromage frais**

**25 g/1 oz caviar**

**thinly sliced white bread, cut into 'soldiers'**

Boil the eggs for 4 minutes. Remove the tops of the shells with a sharp knife, transfer the eggs to egg cups and spoon 1 teaspoon of soured cream or fromage frais into each.

Add 15 g/½ oz caviar to each egg and serve immediately with 'soldiers' of thin white bread (toasted if preferred). Also have available freshly squeezed orange juice and pink champagne.

Serves 2

## Variation
# THE SOPHISTICATED DINNER VERSION

Carefully saw the tops off four free range eggs, empty the contents of the shells into a bowl. Carefully wash out the egg shells and dry or drain on kitchen paper. Place the dry shells into egg cups.

Beat the eggs together and then strain through a sieve to remove any particles of shell or other bits.

Pour the egg mixture into a nonstick pan and over a low heat whisk until the eggs thicken slightly.

Remove the pan from the heat. Stirring continuously add salt and pepper, 2 teaspoons of fromage frais, 1 teaspoon of chopped onion and 1 teaspoon of finely chopped chives. Fill each egg shell with the cooked egg mixture until three-quarters full. Add 15 g/½ oz of caviar to each egg and pop the egg shell tops on top. Serve with wedges of thin white toast.

Serves 4

# SCRAMBLED EGGS WITH CAVIAR

This makes a delicious brunch dish or dinner party starter, it can be served in ramekins as we suggest here or directly onto a plate, whichever suits the occasion.

**25 g/1 oz butter**

**6 eggs**

**1 generous tablespoon double cream**

**50 g/2 oz Sevruga caviar**

**salt and pepper**

Heat four ramekins in a low oven. In a nonstick saucepan gently heat the butter. Place the eggs in a bowl with seasoning to taste - adding salt sparingly as the caviar will be salty. Whisk until frothy, add to the pan and increase the heat slightly. Stir with a wooden spoon until the eggs begin to thicken. Then add the cream. Remove the pan from the heat, still stirring to obtain a thick but creamy consistency. (Adding cream at the end of cooking stops the eggs becoming overcooked and solid.) Transfer to the warm ramekins. Top each portion of scrambled egg with a teaspoon of caviar at the last minute. Serve with hot crisp white toast.

Serves 4

**Variation**

# SCRAMBLED EGGS ON BRIOCHE TOAST

### WITH BELUGA CAVIAR

This makes a luxury breakfast for a special occasion.

Scramble the eggs as in the recipe for Scrambled Eggs with Caviar (above), and spoon on to hot brioche toast. Other forms of bread may be used if preferred, but toasted brioche has a crunchy texture that is perfect with scrambled egg. Serve with Bucks Fizz, made with chilled fresh orange juice and champagne.

Serves 4

According to EEC regulations real caviar has to be
spelt with a 'C' and the cheap imitation with a 'K'.

## CAVIAR WITH QUAILS' EGGS

Simply delicious – if you want a more substantial dish, add some smoked salmon.

**Per Portion**

**3 quails' eggs**

**I teaspoon finely snipped chives**

**1-2 tablespoons fromage frais**

**pinch of ground pepper**

**triangles of hot toast**

**25 g/I oz caviar**

**2 thin wedges of lemon, to garnish**

Bring a saucepan of water to the boil. Put the quails' eggs carefully into a wire basket, lower the basket into the water and boil for 2 minutes.

Drain the eggs and immediately cool them under cold running water. Drain again and gently tap the eggs all around to break the shells. Peel carefully and set aside to cool completely.

Stir the snipped chives into the fromage frais with a pinch of ground pepper. Just before serving arrange the eggs and toast triangles on individual plates. Spoon the fromage frais mixture over the eggs to coat.

Place the caviar and lemon wedges on the plates and serve with a Laurent-Perrier Cuvée Alexandre.

# CANAPÉS

Caviar on canapés is fun and versatile. It can be as impressive or simple as you wish.

You can let your imagination run from simple toast, puff pastry shapes, mini pizzas with crème fraîche,

small new or tiny scooped out baked potatoes...or try one of the recipes below.

The quantities given for these canapés are designed to be flexible, you can simply multiply them to make

just the quantity you need.

### Smoked Salmon with Crème Fraîche and Caviar

Slice across enough smoked salmon fillets and then shape the fillet portions around in circles or mini-

cornets, on toast. Pipe a little crème fraîche on top and add a small spoonful of caviar.

There is an excellent Swiss fillet of smoked salmon called Balik, if you can obtain it.

### Quails Eggs with Keta

Put six quails' eggs into a saucepan of cold water. Bring to the boil and cook for 3 minutes, then drain the

eggs and immediately cool them under cold running water. Remove the shells and carefully cut the eggs in

half. Toast some bread and cut into 12 small rounds or squares with pastry cutters. Peel a 5 cm/2 inch

length of cucumber, slice thinly, cut the slices in half. Arrange half a cucumber slice on each toast round

or square, balance half a quails egg on top and spoon keta (salmon eggs) or caviar on top of each egg.

### Hidden Assets

Take some finely sliced smoked salmon and cut it into rough squares.

Put ½ teaspoon fromage frais and ½ teaspoon Oscietre caviar into the centre of each square, gather up

into a treasure bag and tie with two chives.

### Lobster Tail with Caviar

Cut a cooked lobster tail into slices. Lightly toast as much white bread as you need and cut it into rounds, with a small pastry cutter. Place a slice of lobster (or two) on each toast round.

Top with a few grains of caviar. Alternatively, pop one keta egg (salmon egg) on top with some snipped chives.

### Mangetout

As the title says: you can eat every morsel of these tasty filled vegetables.

Buy the smallest mangetout you can find. Blanch them in a saucepan of boiling water for 30 seconds, then drain, refresh under cold running water and pat dry on kitchen paper. Trim, split open down one side and fill with fromage frais and caviar.

In 1927 Cartier had in their brochure a caviar taster which was a small gold or crystal ball decorated with stars. This was intended to be kept on a watch chain and whenever caviar was served you dropped the ball into it. If the ball sank to the bottom you judged it good and if it stayed in the middle you sent it back!

# CHILLED CAVIAR VICHYSSOISE

Make the vichyssoise the day before you need it, or use a good quality bought vichyssoise.

**50 g/2 oz butter**

**6 large leeks, white parts only, washed, trimmed and finely sliced**

**4 white onions, thinly sliced**

**900 ml/1½ pints water**

**900 ml/1½ pints clear chicken stock**

**6 potatoes, about 175 g/6 oz each, cut in large dice**

**500 ml/17 fl oz double cream**

**½ teaspoon salt**

**2 tablespoons finely snipped chives**

**1 teaspoon lemon juice**

**150 ml/¼ pint soured cream**

**50 g/2 oz Oscietre caviar**

**freshly ground white pepper**

Melt the butter in a large saucepan, add the leeks and onions and cook gently for 10 minutes, stirring occasionally, until the vegetables are soft but not coloured.

Add the measured water, chicken stock and potatoes. Bring to the boil, then lower the heat and simmer for 15-20 minutes until the potatoes are almost tender. Add the double cream and simmer for 5 minutes.

Purée the contents of the pan in a blender or food processor, then press through a sieve into a large bowl. Add the salt, with pepper to taste. Allow to cool, then cover and refrigerate for at least 2 hours.

Just before serving stir in the snipped chives and lemon juice. Pour the soup into eight dishes, add a dollop of soured cream to each and top with a teaspoon of caviar.

Serves 8

# MOUSSELINE OF CAVIAR, SALMON AND HAKE

300 g/10 oz salmon fillets, skinned

250 g/8 oz hake fillets, skinned

2 egg whites

250 ml/8 fl oz double cream

50 g/2 oz Beluga or Oscietre caviar

Tomato Coulis (see page 63)

salt and freshly ground black pepper

Pick over the fish to make sure that all the bones have been removed, then cut into chunks and purée with the egg whites in a blender or food processor. Stop the appliance at frequent intervals to clear the blades and ensure that the mixture at the sides is brought to the centre. When the purée is smooth, rub it through a fine sieve into a bowl set in crushed ice. Add salt and pepper to taste.

Gradually beat in the cream, adding about a spoonful at a time. (This can be done in a food processor but be careful not to overwork the mixture or it will separate.) Chill the mixture in the refrigerator for 20-30 minutes, to thicken slightly.

Butter 6 ramekins or timbale moulds and, using a teaspoon, half fill them with the mixture. Then, using the back of the spoon, make a dent in the mixture and fill with caviar. (If you have any caviar left over, save it for adding to the sauce.) Spoon the rest of the fish mixture carefully into the mould to cover the caviar, turning the mould around as you fill it to just below the rim. Wrap the moulds individually in clingfilm. Put the wrapped moulds in a saucepan large enough to hold them in a single layer. Pour in enough boiling water to come about three quarters of the way up the moulds. Simmer for exactly 8 minutes – no longer or you will cook the caviar!

To serve, invert the cooked mousselines on to eight serving plates and surround with tomato coulis.

*Serves 6*

# SEVRUGA CAVIAR TOPPED POTATO PANCAKES

When it's dark and the weather is bad, potato pancakes topped with salmon and caviar or quails' eggs make a sublime starter, brunch or supper dish - nutritious and not too heavy. The quantities given are for one; simply double or quadruple them to serve two or four.

**1 small potato, about 125 g/4 oz**

**¼ red onion, grated**

**1 egg yolk**

**olive oil for frying**

**salt and pepper**

Topping

**2 tablespoons crème fraîche**

**50 g/2 oz smoked salmon, diced**

**1 or 2 quails' eggs**

**20 g/¾ oz Sevruga caviar**

Peel the potato and grate raw into a bowl. Add the onion and egg yolk, with salt and pepper to taste; mix well. Heat a little olive oil in a frying pan. Using all the potato mixture form two potato pancakes (like a hamburger). Fry in the oil over a low heat for 5-8 minutes on each side, until golden brown. Remove from the pan and drain on kitchen paper. Transfer the pancakes to a plate and keep warm, but not too hot. Spread one potato pancake generously with the crème fraîche and top with the diced smoked salmon. Heat a little more oil in a small frying pan. Carefully break the quails' egg or eggs into the pan. Fry the eggs, they will cook very rapidly and should be served with runny yolks. Put the egg or eggs on the remaining pancake. Divide the caviar evenly between both the pancakes. Serve immediately.

Serves 1

# SMOKED SALMON WITH FRENCH BEAN SALAD
## AND SEVRUGA CAVIAR

300 g/10 oz fillet of smoked salmon (preferably Balik)

150 g/5 oz French beans, trimmed

1 tablespoon wine vinegar

1 tablespoon lemon juice

8 tablespoons olive oil

2 shallots, finely chopped

100 g/3½ oz Sevruga Caviar

salt and pepper

Cut the salmon crossways into thin slices, allowing three pieces per person. Set aside. Blanch the French

beans in a saucepan of boiling water, drain, refresh under cold water and dry on kitchen paper.

To make the dressing, whisk the vinegar and lemon juice together in a salad bowl. Gradually whisk in the

olive oil, with salt and pepper to taste.

Add the shallots. Cut the beans in half and add them to the salad bowl, tossing to coat them in the

dressing. Cover and marinate for 30 minutes to bring out the flavour and allow the onion to soften.

Using a slotted spoon, mound the bean mixture on to one half or in the centre of eight individual plates.

Compliment each plate of beans with three pieces of salmon. Just before serving add a small teaspoonful

of caviar to each salmon slice.

Serves 8

The Swiss and the French eat the most caviar:
the Swiss because they think they should,
and the French because they love it.

## SPAGHETTI WITH CAVIAR AND ASPARAGUS

1 tablespoon oil

500 g/1 lb spaghetti

20 g/¾ oz butter

150 ml/¼ pint single cream

250 g/8 oz asparagus spears (frozen asparagus is fine), sliced

250 g/8 oz smoked salmon, cut into small pieces

50 g/2 oz Sevruga caviar

salt and pepper

Bring a large saucepan of water to the boil, adding a teaspoon of salt and a tablespoon of oil. Cook the spaghetti for 8-12 minutes or until *al dente*.

While the pasta is cooking, make the sauce. Heat the butter, cream and asparagus in a nonstick saucepan. Add salt and pepper to taste. Bring to simmering point and turn off the heat. Stir in the salmon.

Drain the pasta in a colander. Tip it into a bowl and add the sauce. Toss lightly. Top with caviar and serve at once, preferably with a rough country bread.

*Serves 4*

# SANDWICH WITH PRESSED CAVIAR AND CRAB

12 slices of thin white bread

125 g/4 oz pressed caviar

220 g/7½ oz crab meat, preferably Russian whole crab meat (Chatka Crab Royal)

6 tablespoons crème fraîche

6 dill sprigs

lemon slices

Lightly toast the bread. Spread the pressed caviar thinly onto the toast; trim off the edges neatly.

Top six of the slices of toast with pieces of the whole crab meat. (This can be a delicate operation needing some care and attention, to keep the crab meat pieces whole.) Top the crab meat toast with the remaining toast spread with caviar, caviar-side up.

Garnish each sandwich with a tablespoon of crème fraîche, a few dill sprigs and a slice of lemon. Serve immediately or the toast may go soggy.

Serves 6

'Fresh caviar, with its exquisite taste,
needs no further seasoning'
*Ma Cuisine* Auguste Escoffier

# CAVIAR SURPRISE

Spinach parcels filled with fish reveal a surprise filling of caviar when cut. You can serve this as a starter, or as a main course with rice and perhaps stir-fried mangetout and baby corn to add colour and sweetness. We like the tangy wine and butter sauce as it is, but you may prefer to cook and purée any remaining spinach and add this to the sauce.

**4 fillets of lemon sole**

**8-12 large spinach leaves (see method)**

**75 g/3 oz butter**

**50 g/2 oz Sevruga caviar or pressed caviar**

**Tangy Wine and Butter Sauce (see page 63)**

**freshly ground black pepper**

Slice each lemon sole fillet lengthways down the centre, then cut in half crossways to give 16 pieces. (Trim off all the ends and add to the sauce.)

Bring a large saucepan of water to the boil. Wash the spinach leaves well, and trim them to remove any tough stalk ends. Blanch eight large leaves (or more, if the leaves are not large) for a few seconds. Immediately drain and plunge into cold water to prevent overcooking. When cool, dry on kitchen paper. Preheat the oven to 220°C (425°F), Gas Mark 7. Melt the butter in a small saucepan and add generous amounts of pepper. Using a pastry brush, butter the sole on both sides. Reserve the remaining butter. Take a piece of sole and gently spread it with caviar; place another piece of sole on top to make a sandwich. Then wrap this in a blanched spinach leaf to make a parcel. Use the reserved butter to grease an ovenproof dish large enough to hold all the parcels in a single layer. Place the finished parcel in the dish, then make seven more parcels in the same way. Cover the dish with foil and bake for 10-15 minutes, until the sole is cooked through. Divide the parcels between four plates, pour over the sauce and serve.

Serves 4

# SEA BASS WITH A CREAM AND CAVIAR SAUCE

750 g/1½ lb fillets of sea bass or sturgeon, skinned

150 ml/¼ pint fish stock or water

125 ml/4 fl oz dry white wine

500 g/1 lb fresh pasta, preferably tagliolini or linguini

parsley sprigs, to garnish

Sauce

450 ml/¾ pint double or whipping cream

250 g/8 oz unsalted butter, diced

juice of ½ lemon

25 g/1 oz Sevruga caviar

salt and pepper

Place the sea bass or sturgeon in a shallow pan. Add the fish stock or water with the wine and a pinch of salt. Bring gently to simmering point, then remove from the heat, cover and allow to stand for 5 minutes. Bring a large saucepan of salted water to boiling point, so that it is ready to receive the pasta after you have made the sauce.

Heat the cream in the top of a double boiler. As soon as it comes to the boil, remove from the heat and briskly whisk in the cold diced butter, a little at a time. When the sauce is smooth add the lemon juice and season with salt and pepper. Keep the sauce hot over simmering water.

Add the pasta to the pan of salted water. Cook, stirring from time to time to prevent the pasta from sticking, until it is *al dente* or according to the packet recommendations (about 4 minutes). Drain well and then mound on four individual plates. Stir the caviar gently into the sauce and pour over the pasta. Drain the sea bass and add a portion to each plate. Garnish with parsley and serve with a crisp dry white wine.

Serves 4

# SEAFOOD SALAD WITH CAVIAR

8 small new potatoes

2 small cooked lobsters, weighing about 500 g/1 lb each

butter, for frying (optional)

½ garlic clove, chopped (optional)

2 tablespoons white wine vinegar

6 tablespoons light olive oil

about 250 g/8 oz mixed salad leaves

250 g/8 oz smoked salmon

50 g/2 oz Sevruga caviar

8 tiny cherry tomatoes, halved

50 g/2 oz Keta (salmon eggs)

1 tablespoon chopped dill

salt and pepper

Cook the potatoes in boiling salted water for 10 minutes or until tender. Drain and cool, then cut in half.

Shell the cooked lobster, discarding the intestinal tract. Remove the tail and claw meat.

Serve the lobster cold, or sauté gently in a little melted butter and garlic for about 2 minutes. Take out of

the pan with a slotted spoon and allow to cool on kitchen paper. Whisk the vinegar, salt and pepper in a

bowl. Gradually whisk in the oil. Toss the salad leaves in this dressing.

On each plate arrange a thin layer of dressed salad leaves. Cut the smoked salmon into ribbons with sharp

kitchen scissors and arrange on top of the salad. Place the lobster meat around the rim of each plate.

Arrange the potato halves in between and top them with the Sevruga caviar. Garnish with the tomatoes.

Spoon a quarter of the keta into the centre of each plate and sprinkle dill all over. Serve immediately.

Serves 4

# SMOKED SALMON AND CAVIAR PANCAKE

Halfway between a pancake and an omelette, this makes an ideal light dish when served with a fresh green

salad and hot pitta bread.

**250 ml/8 fl oz single cream**

**75 g/3 oz plain flour, sifted**

**6 eggs**

**125 g/4 oz butter**

**250 g/8 oz thinly sliced smoked salmon**

**100 g/3½ oz Oscietre caviar**

**freshly ground black pepper**

To garnish

**8 very thin lemon slices**

**fresh dill**

**soured cream**

Preheat the oven to 200°C (400°F), Gas Mark 6. In a heavy mixing bowl or a food processor, beat the

cream, flour and pepper until smooth, then add one egg at a time, beating vigorously until creamy.

In a 20 cm/8 inch omelette pan with an ovenproof handle, melt the butter over a low heat. Pour in the

batter and cook for 2 minutes, then transfer the pan to the oven and cook until set, about 8 minutes.

Remove the pancake from the oven, cover with some of the smoked salmon and trim. Cut it into eight

slices and put a thin slice of lemon on each. Arrange on four plates. Cut the remaining smoked salmon

into ribbons and arrange around the slices. Make two oval mounds of caviar on each plate, using two non-

metallic teaspoons. Garnish the salmon with a little dill. Serve with soured cream on the side.

Serves 4

# SMOKED OR RAW SALMON TARTARE WITH CAVIAR

This can be made with raw salmon, but unless you are absolutely sure of your source, it is safer to use smoked salmon.

**125 g/4 oz smoked or fresh salmon**

**1 lemon or lime**

**1 red onion, finely chopped**

**30 rinsed capers, drained and chopped**

**125 ml/4 fl oz soured cream**

**12 chicory leaves (optional)**

**50 g/2 oz caviar**

**salt and pepper**

**dill sprigs, to garnish**

Cut the salmon into small dice. With a paring knife cut off strips of rind from the lemon or lime, avoiding the pith. Cut the rind into julienne strips and blanch in boiling water for a few seconds. Drain, rinse under cold water to retain the colour and drain again. Set aside. Squeeze the juice from the lemon or lime into a 600 ml/1 pint pudding bowl; add the salmon, onion, capers and soured cream, with salt and pepper to taste. Mix well, cover and refrigerate for 30 minutes.

Place a serving plate upside down on the pudding bowl mould. Hold both firmly together, then turn right way up and carefully lift off the bowl to reveal the moulded salmon mixture. Arrange the chicory leaves around the mould, if using. Just before serving, garnish with the caviar, lime or lemon strips and dill.

*Serves 4*

# TANGY WINE AND BUTTER SAUCE

1 tablespoon chopped shallot

15 black peppercorns

100 ml/3½ fl oz dry white wine

2 teaspoons white wine vinegar

2 teaspoons double cream

cayenne pepper, to taste

75 g/3 oz chilled butter, diced

Combine the shallots, peppercorns, wine and vinegar in a pan, with any leftover fish. Boil until reduced by half. Add the cream and reduce again. Strain into a bowl. Place the bowl in a pan of hot water, add a little cayenne. When hot gradually whisk in the butter until the sauce is warm, but never boiling, and smooth.

Serves 4

# TOMATO COULIS

75 g/3 oz butter, of which 50 g/2 oz to be diced and kept cold

2 shallots, finely chopped

500 g/1 lb tomatoes, skins removed and chopped

125 ml/4 fl oz fish stock

125 ml/4 fl oz white wine

salt and white pepper

Gently soften the butter and shallots over a low heat. Add the tomatoes and cook for 1 minute. Add the stock, wine, salt and pepper and simmer for 20 minutes. When the sauce has cooled rub it through a sieve. When required re-heat and whisk in the cold butter, until all the butter has melted.

Serves 4